PARIS

CITY OF LIGHT

PARIS

CITY OF LIGHT

MIMMO JODICE

MAISON EUROPÉENNE DE LA PHOTOGRAPHIE

APERTURE

This publication is made possible by the collaboration of

Emblematic Italian photographer Mimmo Jodice looks at Paris in a metaphysical manner. Harmoniously combining a historical and a modern vision, he gives us here, at the dawn of the third millenium, a new iconography. The City of Light offers herself not only with her most prestigious symbols—the Louvre, Notre Dame, the Seine, the museums—but also in her most contemporary aspects which, in the last fifteen years, have made of the French capital a great European metropolis.

Through the images featured in this book, Mimmo Jodice joins the prestigious lineage of the city's photographers who, like Marville or Atget, have known how to celebrate, through their art, Paris and her metamorphoses.

JEAN-LUC MONTEROSSO
Director, Maison Européenne de la Photographie

SPYING ON GHOSTS   *ADAM GOPNIK*

PARIS TODAY IS A PLACE that has been not so much seen as scoured, strip-mined for sights. The parks and boulevards that once belonged to Degas and Manet now have been left to the Sunday amateurs with their over-loaded colors; whole *arrondissements* are left to the postcard makers. Photographers require more elbow room, but they're just as crowded as the rest of us, with their old haunts inhabited by the black-and-white ghosts of Atget and Cartier-Bresson. The temptation is to go off and look at Prague or Perth Amboy.

Love of Paris, though, remains one of the strongest emotions many of us possess, and those who do usually pass through a kind of double gainer dive on the way toward a new vision of the place. First comes the rejection of the merely familiar "touristic" Paris: great monuments, children in parks, the Eiffel Tower looming everywhere. It becomes a form of snobbery to insist that the "real" Paris is Somewhere Else. This produces in turn many terrifying, parallax-view photographs of La Défense or the Montparnasse Tower, and, among writers, long articles about Algerian rappers in the suburbs.

This Paris, too, has elements of a cliché; the idea of a real Paris that exists outside the familiar Paris is itself a very Parisian idea, which takes one back at least to the painters of the "Zone" in the 1880s—that no-man's wasteland just outside the city, beloved of the Neo-Impressionists. (Paris has always depended on a ring around the city that feeds and houses the center. In the old days, with Les Halles around, Paris worked northward from the belly up to the head and heart. But now it works from the periphery inward, with hideous skyscrapers—no other city in the world has less hold on verticality—and ugly ring roads that connect the suburbs to the main city.)

The challenge of making a real picture of Paris by avoiding the tourist traps becomes in itself a kind of tourist trap. So then one returns to the familiar Paris, swearing to see it fresh, to see it for oneself. Only to have the ghosts come swarming back.

The wise thing is to surrender to the familiar, but to surrender on French terms; i.e., pretending that you haven't. Mimmo Jodice's pictures of Paris have an air of subterfuge and espionage, as though Notre Dame, seen from the back of the boat, were a secret nuclear installation; as though St. Eustache, glimpsed over the top of the Forum des Halles, were something sinister, whose purpose is hidden from view. It is a Paris without figures but rife with the traces of people. The little corporal's hat and coat—with the corporal himself gone missing. The empty metro station—with its melancholy angles meeting like those on a de Chirico street.

Often one sees Paris in these pictures through long alleys and arcades, so that even the Parisian resident thinks, "My goodness, look at that! A man rising on horseback at the end of the street!" When of course, it is just old Louis, in the Place des Victoires, which you pass every evening on the way to a steak *béarnaise*.

The spy's sense of accelerated time is there too: the carousel near the Trocadéro spins around in a blur as we dash up toward the Arc de Triomphe and then around, right toward the hideous necessity of La Défense. These photographs speed to an essential truth, which is that Paris is kindest to those who do not look at it directly, head on. One way to transform the touristic Paris into the permanent Paris it contains is to see it on the run. Paris is cruel to people who come to Paris for "Paris." You see them crowded mournfully on the tour boats and in the bad restaurants of the Sixth arrondissement. But give yourself a reason—another purpose, *any* purpose, something to set your teeth for—and suddenly the city, as in these pictures, comes to wonderful life: "I have to be in the Eighth arrondissement, by three o'clock," and then, "My God, is this the Place de la Concorde?" A secret known only to Americans in Paris who run round the Luxembourg Garden, morning after morning, hideous in track pants and "Tanglewood" sweat-shirts, is that the great advantage of doing this is not just what it does for your lungs but what it does for your eyes. Of all the pictures in this book, it is perhaps those of the Luxembourg Garden that especially move an American refugee in Paris—the two empty chairs by the sand-box, the *marronniers* lined up like guards at attention, watching the watcher. As you run past, legs pumping, lungs working, the statues and pavilions of the Garden seem like a great joke.

Mimmo Jodice's photographs remind us of the central lesson of the Impressionists in Paris: that pompous places can be transformed into poetry by speed and an eccentric glance. Even that most pompous of all official buildings, the National Assembly—which joins the Boulevard St. Germain and the Quai d'Orsay like an ostentatious hinge on a bourgeois door—even that looks good here, reduced by Jodice to a little Greek pediment peeking up over the Seine. Jodice demonstrates that glory looks best at a very great distance, and official beauty looks best from a moving bus.

It is the light, of course, that brings it all together. The émigré to Paris quickly discovers however, that the light the Impressionists celebrated is the hardest to find. Painters threw a party when they saw that light because they didn't see it often. The light in Paris is silk-violet, pearl gray—most often the good gray that suffuses Manet's interiors, not the rare lemon-yellow that he saw outside. This light, diffused in spring, the light of a snowstorm that is always just about to happen, is a black-and-white light, and it fills Jodice's pictures, bringing with it a smell—that Parisian smell of fireplaces and strong cigarettes and steamed milk—that magically fills the images.

The necessary lesson at the end of the book, at the end of time in the city, is that it is the touristic Paris—the Paris of the Pyramide, the gardens, carousels, even the Trocadéro and the Arc de Triomphe—that is the real, or anyway the necessary Paris, the one we need. For the touristic Paris is cosmopolitan Paris, and it is cosmopolitan Paris that matters most. The Paris that was still so crazy about ideas that it made a whole city out of them—despite being forced into life in this little gray corner of Northern Europe, too cold, really, and too damp, with too long a winter and too late a spring.

We love Paris because each of its sites seems to sum up a whole state of mind, with the contradictions and clichés that the mind contains. In the rushing Champs-Elysées we find an idea of Glory, in the empty hall of the Louvre an idea of Art, and everywhere else we are encompassed by an idea of Pleasure. In Paris, we turn the tables on the phantoms, who try to make us their slaves, by making them our subject.

14 *Palais de Chaillot* / Palais de Chaillot

16 ABOVE: *Hôtel des Invalides* / Hôtel des Invalides RIGHT: *St-Denis* / St. Denis Abbey

L'AMPHION *Raymond Queneau, 1943*

Le Paris que vous aimâtes
n'est pas celui que nous aimons
et nous nous dirigeons sans hâte
vers celui que nous oublierons

Topographies! itinéraires!
dérives à travers la ville!
souvenirs des anciens horaires!
que la mémoire est difficile . . .

Et sans un plan sous les yeux
on ne nous comprendra plus
car tout ceci n'est que jeu
et l'oubli d'un temps perdu

AMPHION

The Paris you loved
is not the same one that we love
and unhurriedly we're heading now
toward the one we shall forget

Topographies! and travel plans!
spin-offs all across the town!
remembering the schedules of before!
how difficult remembrance is . . .

And without a map before our eyes
we shall not be understood
for all of this is but a game
and the neglect of time gone by

ABOVE: *Musée Rodin* / Musée Rodin PAGE 20: *La Grande Halle de La Villette* / The Grand Hall at La Villette PAGE 21: *Cité Universitaire* / Cité Universitaire 19

22 *Palais de Tokyo* / Tokyo Palace

Eustache Deschamps, 1375

C'est la cité sur toutes couronnée
Fontaine et puits de science et de clergie
Sur le fleuve de Seine située
Vigne, bois, terres et prairies;
De tous les biens de cette mortelle vie
A plus qu'autres cite's n'ont,
Tous les étrangers l'aiment et ameront
Car pour déduit et pour être jolie
Jamais cité telle ne trouveront,
Rien ne se peût comparer à Paris.

This is the city crowned above all others
Fountain of science and of clergy too
Seated on the river Seine with
Vineyard, woods,
  expanse of land, and meadows;
More than any other city
She offers all that's good in this
  impermanent life,
Every foreigner loves her now and always will
For to encounter merriment and loveliness
No such city ever will they find,
Nothing to Paris can ever be compared.

LEFT: *Le Parc Monceau* / Monceau Park ABOVE: *Musée du Louvre* / The Louvre 27

de AU COEUR DU MONDE
Blaise Cendrars, 1967

Dans cette lumière froide et crue,
　tremblotante, plus qu'irréelle,
Paris est comme l'image refroidie d'une plante
Qui réapparaît dans sa cendre. Triste simulacre,
Tirées au cordeau et sans age,
　les maisons et les rues ne sont
Que pierre et fer en tas dans un désert
　invraisemblable.

---

from IN THE WORLD'S HEART

In this hard cold light, trembling, more than unreal,
Paris is like the frozen image of a plant
That reappears in its ashes. A sad simulacrum.
Linear, ageless, the buildings and streets are only
Stone and steel, heaped up, an unlikely desert.

30 *Beaubourg* / Beaubourg

Stalingrad / Stalingrad

de À L'INTERIEUR DU PERIPHERIQUE

Il me semble parfois que Paris marque
le passage du temps. Émergeant d'un passé
récent sans trop de gloire, pour ainsi dire, il se
prépare à un avenir auquel il semble déjà
beaucoup mieux adapté que toutes les autres
villes. Peut-être que l'horloge numérique du
Centre Pompidou, qui égrène les secondes
qui nous séparent de la fin du siècle, fait le
compte à rebours de Paris lui-même; peut-être
que les escaliers mécaniques, les ascenseurs
et les tapis roulants, qui sont déjà les plus
rapides du monde, accélèrent d'année en
année pour accoutumer les parisiens au rythme
du millénaire.

from WITHIN THE PERIPHERIQUE *Jan Morris, 1992*

Sometimes it seems to me that Paris is marking
time. Emerging from a recent past without,
not to put too fine a point upon it, all that
much honor, it is girding itself for a future
to which it already seems much better attuned
than most of its peers. Perhaps the Centre
Pompidou digital clock, ticking away the
seconds towards the end of the century, is
counting down for the city itself; perhaps the
escalators, elevators, and walkways, which
already move faster here than they do else-
where in the world, are being imperceptibly
speeded up, year by year, to accustom
Parisians to the pace of the millennium.

de Le Futurisme
Filippo Tommaso Marinetti, 1909

Nous sommes sur le promontoire extrême des siècles! . . .
A quoi bon regarder derrière nous, du moment qu'il
nous faut défoncer les vantaux mystérieux de
l'Impossible? Le Temps et l'Espace sont morts hier.
Nous vivons déjà dans l'absolu, puisque nous avons
déjà créé l'éternelle vitesse omniprésente.

from the Manifesto of Futurism

We stand on the last promontory of the centuries! . . .
Why should we look back, when what we want is to
break down the mysterious doors of the Impossible?
Time and Space died yesterday. We already live
in the absolute, because we have created eternal,
omnipresent speed.

La Défense /
La Défense

50 *Quai de Bercy* / Quai de Bercy

52 *Beaubourg* / Beaubourg

de LE CIGNE *Charles Baudelaire, 1861*

Paris change! mais rien dans ma mélancolie
N'a bougé! palais neufs, échafaudages, blocs,
Vieux faubourgs, tout pour moi devient allégorie,
Et mes chers souvenirs sont plus lourds que des rocs.

---

from THE SWAN

Paris changes, but nothing of my melancholy
Gives way. Foundations, scaffoldings, tackle, and blocks,
And the old suburbs drift off into allegory,
While my frailest memories take on the weight of rocks.

56 *Musée Rodin* / Musée Rodin

ABOVE: *Jardin du Luxembourg* / The Luxembourg Garden PAGE 60: *Les Invalides* / Les Invalides PAGE 61: *Intérieur* / Interior 59

62 *Palais de Tokyo* / Tokyo Palace

de PARIS Julian Green, 1983

Ici peut-être, à l'endroit même où je me tiens,
un Barbare a rêvé aux hommes de l'avenir.
Et moi, je songe à ce Paris futur, élevé sur
l'espace qui est le nôtre, et où le béton brut,
le verre, l'acier, et peut-être d'autres matériaux
inconnus encore, seront les éléments d'une
beauté sans fin.

from PARIS

Maybe on this very spot where I am standing
a Barbarian mused about the men that were to
come. And here am I, dreaming of that Paris of
the future, raised up on the space that is now
ours, where shuttered concrete, glass, steel, and
possibly other materials as yet unknown will be
the ingredients of a limitless beauty.

70 *St-Sulpice* / St. Sulpice

To Angela, who lovingly endures the tensions
and discomforts that all my works bring.

AN ILLUSTRATED GUIDE TO PARIS *MIMMO JODICE*

PARIS AND THE EIFFEL TOWER. There are places to which we no longer know how to react: how to observe them, go through them, live them. How to bear the overdose of sophisticated images or instant shots that reach us daily, wherever we might be, from Paris or other renowned places, reassuring us that the "City of Light" is still there, still the same, still available.

When I began this visual trip I felt the need not to avoid the "commonplace." I felt the need to joust with the Louvre and the Eiffel Tower, the Beaubourg and the Trocadéro, the Seine and Les Invalides, so as to understand how I should see again these superficial icons, thus freeing them from the sacral and commercial aura that fetters them. In this trip I also encountered a fin de siècle *Metropolis* and a postmodern Paris that seem to have entered a dialogue with the historical Paris in a very uninhibited and aggressive way. With the same lack of inhibition I mixed images from these two Parisian souls in a sort of encounter that is also a confrontation. Because they are anonymous, they are all the same. These places of confrontation are commonplace in this third-millenium Babel.

This work aspires to be a kind of *Illustrated Guide to Paris* where every place, ancient or modern, is seen as if in a first showing. I tried to describe a Paris that, albeit shown in all its familiarity, is difficult to recognize. These pictures generate, perhaps, a sense of unease, of not belonging; thereby they attempt to exorcise the postcard fiction that inhibits us from experiencing certain cities. Photographs to make the commonplace new again: Paris and the Eiffel Tower.

ACKNOWLEDGEMENTS

All the photographs reproduced in this book were taken in 1993–1994.

My sincere thanks and affection to Jean-Luc Monterosso who wanted and supported this work. My thanks also to all the staff at the Maison Européenne de la Photographie.

Special thanks to Umberto Esposito of Agip Petroli for the unremitting care he gave my work.

An affectionate mention to my good friends Fernando Caruso, Anna Civalleri, Anna Rosa and Giovanni Cotroneo, Jean Digne, Maria Carla and Antonio Guarneri, Bernard Miller, Luciana Miotto, Laura Serani, Silvana Turzio, and Paola and Lucio Zagari.

To Michael Hoffman I owe appreciation and gratitude for having once again believed in my work. I also thank all the staff at Aperture, in particular, Stevan Baron, Melissa Harris, Diana Stoll, Phyllis Thompson Reid, and Michelle Dunn.

SELECTED ONE-PERSON EXHIBITIONS

1970   Galleria Il Diaframma, Milan

1975   Galleria Lucio Amelio, Naples

1981   Museo Villa Pignatelli, Naples

1982   Biblioteca Marciana, Venice

1985   Villa Borghese, Rome

1986   Memorial Federal Hall, New York

1988   Istituto Suor Orsola, Naples

1988   Mois de la Photo, Paris

1990   Castel Sant'Elmo, Naples

1991   Galleria Forum, Terragona

1992   Galleria la Nuova Pesa, Rome

1992   Palace "u Hybernu," Prague

1994   Galleria Wan Fung, Pechino

1995   Galleria Lia Rumma, Naples

1995   Philadelphia Museum of Art, Philadelphia

1996   Triennale di Milan, Milan

1996   Museo di Capodimonte, Naples

1996   Galerie du Chateau d'Eau, Toulouse

1997   "Recontres Internazionales de la Photographie," Arles

1997   Galerie Meert Rihoux, Brussels

SELECTED BOOKS AND CATALOGS

Chi e' Devoto (Edizioni scientifiche Italiane, Naples, 1974)

La Napoli di Mimmo Jodice (Progresso fotografico, January 1978)

Vedute di Napoli (Nuove Edizione Gabriele Mazzotta, Milan, 1980)

Naples Une Archeologie Future (I.C.I., Paris, 1982)

Gibellina (Edizione Electa, Milan, 1982)

Mimmo Jodice (Gruppo Editoriale Fabbri, Milan, 1982)

Suor Orsola (Edizioni Mazzotta, Milan, 1987)

Mimmo Jodice Fotografie (Edizioni Electa, Naples, 1988)

Arles (Musée Réattu, Arles, 1988)

La Citté Invisibile (Edizioni Electa, Naples, 1990)

I Percorsi della Memoria (Synchron, Rome, 1990)

Confini (Edizione Incontri Internazionali d'Arte, Rome, 1992)

Passé Interieur (Contrejour, Paris, 1993)

Mediterranean (Aperture, New York, 1995)

Le Avanguardie artistiche a Napoli (Federico Motta Editore, Milan, 1996)

Library of Congress
Catalog Card Number: 97-76792
Hardcover ISBN: 0-89381-792-9

Book design by Michelle M. Dunn
Jacket design by Carol Devine Carson

Printed and bound by L.E.G.O., Vicenza, Italy
Separations by Sele Offset, Turin, Italy

The staff at Aperture for *Paris: City of Light* is:

Michael E. Hoffman, *Executive Director*
Vincent O'Brien, *General Manager*
Stevan A. Baron, *Production Director*
Phyllis Thompson Reid, *Editor*
Lesley A. Martin, *Assistant Editor*
Helen Marra, *Production Manager*
Nell Elizabeth Farrell, Cara Maniaci, *Editorial Assistants*
Steven Garrelts, *Production Assistant*

Aperture Foundation publishes a periodical, books, and portfolios of fine photography to communicate with serious photographers and creative people everywhere. A complete catalog is available upon request. Address: 20 East 23rd Street, New York, NY 10010. Phone: (212) 598-4205. Fax: (212) 598-4015. Toll-free: (800) 929-2323. Visit Aperture's website: http://www.aperture.org.

Aperture Foundation books are distributed internationally through: CANADA: General Publishing, 30 Lesmill Road, Don Mills, Ontario, M3B 2T6. Fax: (416) 445-5991. UNITED KINGDOM, SCANDINAVIA, AND CONTINENAL EUROPE: Robert Hale, Ltd., Clerkenwell House, 45-47 Clerkenwell Green, London EC1R OHT, United Kingdom. Fax: 171-490-4958. NETHERLANDS: Nilsson & Lamm, BV, Pampuslaan 212-214, P.O. Box 195, 1382 JS Weesp. Fax: 31-294-415054.

For international magazine subscription orders for the periodical *Aperture*, contact Aperture International Subscription Service, P.O. Box 14, Harold Hill, Romford, RM3 8EQ, United Kingdom. One year: $50.00. Price subject to change.

To subscribe to the periodical *Aperture* in the U.S.A. write Aperture, P.O. Box 3000, Denville, NJ 07834. Tel: 1-800-783-4903. One year: $40.00. Two years: $66.00.

First edition
10 9 8 7 6 5 4 3 2 1